MW00679301

# THE OFFICIAL RULES OF

# LIFE

# THE OFFICIAL RULES OF

# LIFE

## PAUL DICKSON

**BARNES**
**&NOBLE**
**BOOKS**
NEW YORK

To Andrew and Alex—
May this come in handy.

2000 Barnes & Noble Books

ISBN 0-7607-2049-5

Book design by Tanya Maiboroda

Printed and bound in the United States of America

00 01 02 03 04 MC 9 8 7 6 5 4 3 2 1

QF

# INTRODUCTION

"Always slow down for Dead Man's Curve."

This was the gist of a letter sent to me by a friend, Neal Wilgus, of Lubbock, Texas. He called it Wilgus's Warning and I immediately added it to my ever-growing list of personal rules to live by. For this American male in his late fifties this new warning is a much wittier and more trenchant reminder to diet, exercise, and observe general mid-life moderation than, say, a long list of traditional do's and don'ts. I have posted Wilgus's Warning next to the closet where I keep my walking shoes. It will have other applications too; but I'm not sure when or where.

What I do know is that I will be faced with a choice and my lips will move and I will utter the euphonious mantra Wilgus's Warning.

There are others that I use—many of them—and here is another:

"You have to work quickly and find a niche."

This sits above my desk and has been there since I ripped it out of page 181 of the October 6, 1986, issue of *Forbes*. It was originally used as a photo caption and was not intended as any sort of revealed wisdom. It is a very personal thing telling me that bills have to be paid, that personal productivity counts, and that it is fine to have a specialty (in my case, books about words and the English language).

Then there is this one:

"Remember Hellmann's Principle."

I see this message every morning when I fire up my computer, which has been programmed to deliver it on the screen before I do anything else.

It is a personal reminder of two things: (1) I have been known to get upset during the course of the workday; and (2) once upset I have been known to turn into a Milquetoast to compensate for having gotten upset in the first place. The principle was given to me a few years ago by an artist named A. Peter Hollis, who used it in the same way I do. He discovered it one day while looking at the side of a jar of mayonnaise.

The principle?

"Keep cool but do not freeze."

### GETTING THE MESSAGE

Messages like this are physically displayed all around the spaces where I live and work. Others are tucked away in some fold of my brain and others are filed in cardboard boxes. They are pointed and concise and pass for this individual's attempt to codify and use common sense and not-so-common sense. Most are no longer than eight or nine words and are modern versions of ancient and traditional proverbs.

Wilgus's Warning and Hellmann's Principle are important to me personally, but so too is Agnes Allen's Law, which states:

"Almost anything is easier to get into than out of."

The "anything" applies to everything from arguments, to debt, to installment plans, to committees. It is most useful as a caution. I still serve on committees and other bodies, but I have chosen not to serve on others thanks to this law. It seems like it was created to keep me questioning new levels of involvement which may be superfluous, costly, and/or a bona fide waste of time.

Finally, there is a new rule that has come to my attention which has begun to have a real impact on my life. It is called Smokler's Razor and holds to this truth:

"The secret is not to learn something you don't want to practice."

The item comes from the *Dallas Morning News* in an August 16, 1998, article about a Mrs. Smokler, whose job was to keep the books on a dairy farm, but who had never once milked a cow because she was too smart to learn how. At the very moment that this truth was revealed to me I was in the throes of learning a new system for word processing with a rating of four migraines and a hemorrhoid. Mrs. Smokler gave me the courage to abandon it and opt for the one with which I am writing this.

Finally, if we go to a higher plane there is an admonition which long ago was delivered to me via fortune cookie:

> "The person who says it cannot be done should not interrupt person doing it."

This is how it has been for centuries. We post around us warnings and aphorisms and rules—bits of common sense and conventional wisdom—as small guideposts to help us get through daily life. The only problem is that so much of the traditional advice does not work for people who find themselves trying to live in the dawning hours of the 21st century.

A little background is in order.

It started simply. In 1976 the author of this book created something called the Murphy Center for the Codification of Human and Organizational Law. He appointed himself its first director, and has been, since 1989, its self-appointed director for life. It originally amounted to nothing more than a shoebox into which rules and laws were filed.

The Center was created in an effort to collect, test, and make a few bucks from revealed truth which is often the by-product of what the Center likes to think of fondly as O.F.F.M. & G.C., or Other Folk's Foibles, Misfortunes, and General Confusion. It was mainly inspired by Murphy's Law ("If anything can go wrong it will") and influenced by the fact that we had put men on the moon but still seemed unable to create shoelaces that didn't break at inopportune moments.

The now-esteemed and verging-on-venerable Murphy Center is alive and well and enjoying its perverse nature, which means that it thrives on a little turmoil, bad economic times, and the widespread awareness that the universe is flawed. The Center has published seven books of its findings and has now spread out into eight shoeboxes. Great gobs of its early material have been pirated and put onto Web pages by folks whose only original idea ever was to get access to a copy machine. And so it is, that with this eighth volume of material, the Murphy Center is ready and willing to advance into the new millennium.

The laws that follow appear in the exact language of the person who discovered the phenomenon or universal truth, including their name for that discovery. Every attempt has been made to find the original author of each discovery, but, sadly, some appear as "unknown origin."

The items were collected over a period of years and are listed alphabetically by the name of the law, effect, or principle. This gives them a sense of categorical and chronological randomness that approximates the subjects at hand.

*Abrams's Advice.* When eating an elephant take one bite at a time.

—GENERAL CREIGHTON W. ABRAMS

*Abramson's Law of Bachelorhood.* Always have plenty of underwear.

—JOE ABRAMSON; from Dallas Brozik, Huntington, West Virginia

*Ackley's Second Axiom.* Familiarity breeds attempt. *Ackley's Third Law of Roller Skating.* Everyone spends at least *some* time on the floor (or sidewalk).

—BOB ACKLEY, Plattsmouth, Nebraska

*Adams's Law of Gossip.* Ninety-two percent of the stuff told you in confidence you couldn't get anyone else to listen to.

—Journalist, poet, and humorist FRANKLIN PIERCE ADAMS

*Adams's Laws.* (1) Women don't know what they want; they don't like what they've got. (2) Men know very well what they want; having got it, they begin to lose interest.

—A. W. ADAMS, Magdalen College, Oxford, England

*Addis's Elaboration of Forrest Gump's Simile.* My mama always said life is like a box of chocolates. It disappears before you can get your share. *Addis's Remark on the Current State of Affairs.* Our main social activities are whining and dining.

—DON ADDIS, St. Petersburg, Florida

*Adkin's Rule of Milk and Other Precious Commodities.* The less you have, the more you spill.

—BETSY ADKINS, Gardiner, Maine

*Adlai's Axiom.* He who slings mud generally loses ground.

—ADLAI STEVENSON, 1954

*Adler's Explanation.* Life intrudes.

—Pet expression of acting teacher STELLA ADLER

*Agnes Allen's Law.* Almost anything is easier to get into than out of.

—AGNES ALLEN was the wife of the famous historian Frederick Lewis Allen. When her husband was teaching at Yale University, he encountered an ambitious student named Louis Zahner, who

wanted to create and be remembered for a law of his own.
Zahner worked on it and finally hit upon one that states: "If
you play with anything long enough it will break." Inspired by
his student, Allen then went to work on his own and came up
with *Allen's Law:* "Everything is more complicated than it
looks to most people." Agnes Allen then got into the act and
proceeded to outdistance Zahner and her husband by creating
the law that to this day carries her full name. Frederick Allen
later wrote of his wife's law: " . . . at one stroke human wisdom
had been advanced to an unprecedented degree." All of this was
revealed in a column by Jack Smith in the *Los Angeles Times*
after he had researched the question of who Murphy and Agnes
Allen were. Needless to say, he proved Ms. Allen's law in the
process.

*Air Force Inertia Axiom.*   Consistency is always easier to defend
than correctness.

> —ANONYMOUS; from Russell Fillers, Bethel, Connecticut

*Akre's Axiom.*   Do not readily ascribe to malice what can be
more easily ascribed to incompetence. *Corollary.* Beware of mali-
cious incompetents!

> —JAMES AKRE, Confignon, Switzerland

*Albert's Law of the Sea.* The more they are in a fog, the more boats (and people) toot their horns.

—BERNARD L. ALBERT, M.D., Scarsdale, New York

*Albrecht's Epistolary Effort.* Troublesome correspondence that is postponed long enough will eventually become irrelevant.

—MARK ALBRECHT; from Brooks Alexander, Berkeley, California

*Alderson's Theorem.* If at first you don't succeed, you are running about average.

—M. H. ALDERSON, from the *Lawrence County* [Missouri] *Record*

*Alexander's Rules.* (1) If a wife is happy about the toilet seat, the husband should spend more time at home. (2) Help a man who is in trouble and that man will remember you when he is in trouble again.

—PAUL ALEXANDER, Venice, California

*Alex's Iron Axiom.* Life is the ultimate IQ test.

—ALEX FRASER, Washington, D.C.

*Alfalfa's Observation.* Another day, another zero!

—From T. A. MOORE III, M.D., New Orleans, Louisiana, who recalls it from a memorable scene in the *Our Gang* comedies when Spanky, Buckwheat, and Alfalfa are descending the steps of their school after another day of intellectual disaster.

*Algren's Precepts.* Never eat at a place called Mom's. Never play cards with a man named Doc. And never lie down with a woman who's got more troubles than you.

—NELSON ALGREN, from *What Every Young Man Should Know*

*Allen's Formula.* If you want to be a success in life, just show up 80 percent of the time.

—Writer/actor/director WOODY ALLEN

*Allen's Lament.* Everybody wants to be waited on.

—MARY ALLEN, McLean, Virginia

*Allison's Advice.* It doesn't do any good to put the brakes on when you're upside down.

—Race car driver BOBBY ALLISON after a crash; from Jim
   Murrison, Port Orange, Florida, who suggests that it has a
   wider application beyond car racing

*Amis's Admonition.* You can't believe anyone but yourself, and don't trust yourself too completely.

*Amis's Advice.* Go ahead and be different—if you think you can stand the beating you'll get.

*Amis's Calculation.* Any fool can line up two fence posts. It's when you add the third that it gets tough.

*Amis's Discovery.* There are a lot more cowboy boots than there are cowboys.

*Amis's Famous Saying.* Obesity looks best on fat people.

*Amis's Reminder.* Humor is the reminder that no matter how high the throne one sets on, one sets on one's bottom.
　　　　—JIM AMIS, Springfield, Missouri

*Andersen's Discovery.* It matters not so much whether you do something well or badly, but how you get out of doing it honestly.
　　　　—KURT ANDERSEN in his book *The Real Thing*

*Ann's Law of Inevitability.* You never meet that terrific person until the day before your vacation ends.
　　　　—ANN L. MOORE, Exeter, New Hampshire

*Anonymous's Bodily Discovery.* Whatever doesn't stick out is hanging down.

—Name withheld by request

*Approval Seeker's Law.* Those whose approval you seek the most give you the least.

—Washington writer ROZANNE WEISSMAN

*The Aquinas Axiom.* What the gods get away with, the cows don't.

—DONALD R. WOODS, Stanford, California

*Armor's Axiom of Morality.* Virtue is the failure to achieve vice.

—JOHN C. ARMOR, Baltimore, Maryland

*Armstrong's Collection Law.* If the check is truly in the mail, it is surely made out to someone else.

—JAMES S. ARMSTRONG, San Francisco, California

*Ash's Axiom.* Any request prefaced by the word "just" will be unjust (e.g., This will just take a second; this will just hurt for a moment, etc.)

—BILL ASH, Miami Lakes, Florida

***Atwood's Fourteenth Corollary.*** No books are lost by lending except those you particularly wanted to keep.

>—ALAN ATWOOD, a programmer at the University Computing Center, University of Arizona

***Augustine's Plea.*** Give me chastity and self-restraint, but do not give it yet.

>—SAINT AUGUSTINE

***Austen's Rule of Hospitality.*** One cannot have too large a party.

>—JANE AUSTEN in *Emma*

**Baber's Rule.** Anything worth doing is worth doing in excess.

—SUSAN BABER, St. Louis, Missouri

**Baird's Law.** Sex, like money, is an inexhaustible commodity. The problem is getting others to part with it. *Corollary 1:* Getting others to part with it is exhausting. *Corollary 2:* The other person will become exhausted second.

—J. STACEY BAIRD, Hanover Park, Illinois

**Baker's Byroad.** When you are over the hill, you pick up speed.

—UNKNOWN ORIGIN; from Donald R. Woods, Stanford, California

**Baker's Law.** Misery no longer loves company. Nowadays it insists on it.

—Columnist RUSSELL BAKER

*Balzer's Law.*  Life is what happens to you while you are making other plans.

—ROBERT BALZER

*Banks's Law of Misplaced Objects.*  You always find something in the last place you look for it.

—JIM BANKS, Bozeman, Montana

*Barbara's Law of Exploitation.*  You can't be treated like a doormat if you don't lie down. *Barbara's Rule of Bitter Experience.* (1) When you empty a drawer for his clothes and a shelf for his toiletries, the relationship ends. (2) When you finally buy pretty stationery to continue the correspondence, he stops writing.

—BARBARA K. MEHLMAN, Great Neck, New York

*Baron's Law.*  The world is divided between victims and predators, and you have to defend yourself against both.

—FLORENZ BARON, Carlsbad, California

*Barr's Comment on Domestic Tranquillity.*  On a beautiful day like this it's hard to believe anyone can be unhappy—but we'll work on it.

—DONALD BARR, Highland Park, Illinois.

*Barrymore's Conclusion.* The thing that takes up the least amount of time and causes the most amount of trouble is sex.
> —Actor JOHN BARRYMORE

*Barry's Version of Newton's Law of Gravity.* A dropped object will fall with an acceleration of 32 feet per second per second. And if it is your wallet, it will make every effort to land in a public toilet.
> —Newspaper columnist DAVE BARRY

*Bartel's Law.* When someone is kicking your ass, at least you know when you are out in front.
> —DONALD E. BARTEL, Palo Alto, California

*Bartz's Law of Hokey Horsepuckery.* The more ridiculous a belief system, the higher the probability of its success.
> —WAYNE R. BARTZ, in his article "Keys to Success,"
> *Human Behavior,* May 1975

*Bastl's Law.* If there are two parts to anything, you will always miss the first part.
> —JAMES F. BASTL, Westchester, Illinois (originally published in
> the *Chicago Tribune* on November 20, 1983).

*Bax's Rule.* You should make a point of trying every experience once—except incest and folk dancing.
> —ARNOLD BAX, quoted by Nigel Rees in *Quote . . . Unquote*

*Beauregard's Law.* When you're up to your nose, keep your mouth shut.

> —Uttered by HENRY FONDA in the role of Jack Beauregard in the film *My Name Is Nobody*

*Beifield's Principle.* The probability of a young man meeting a desirable and receptive young female increases by pyramidical progression when he is already in the company of (1) a date, (2) his wife, (3) a better-looking and richer male friend.

> —RONALD H. BEIFIELD, Philadelphia attorney; originally submitted to Alan Otten of the *Wall Street Journal* with this alternative title, *The Law of Inverse Proportion of Social Intercourse*

*Bennett's Beatitudes.* (1) Blessed is he who has reached the point of no return and knows it, for he shall enjoy living. (2) Blessed is he who expects no gratitude, for he shall not be disappointed.

> —W. C. BENNETT, Trinity Avenue Presbyterian Church, Durham, North Carolina

*Bentov's Law.*  One's level of ignorance increases exponentially with accumulated knowledge. For example, when one acquires a bit of new information, there are many new questions that are generated by it, and each new piece of information breeds five or ten new questions. These questions pile up at a much faster rate than does the accumulated information. The more one knows, therefore, the greater his level of ignorance.

—ITSAHAK BENTOV, in *Stalking the Wild Pendulum;*
from Neal Wilgus

*Berla's Version.*  If you file it, you'll never need it. If you need it, you never file it.

—MICHAEL BERLA, Columbia, Maryland

*Berra's Clarification.*  It's déjà vu all over again.

—YOGI BERRA

*Billings's Realization.*  Life consists not in holding good cards, but in playing those we do hold well.

—JOSH BILLINGS (1818–1885)

*Bill's Briefing on Annoying Events.*  One time is an accident. Two times is a coincidence. Three times is an enemy action.

—ANONYMOUS, from Arlen Wilson, San Francisco, California

***Bishop's Definition.***  Tact is the art of telling someone to lose thirty pounds without ever using the word fat.
> —BETTY BISHOP, Chester, California

***Bishop's Theorem.***  When you have accumulated sufficient knowledge to get by, you're too old to remember it.
> —Columnist and author JIM BISHOP

***Black's Discovery.***  He who laughs first, laughs last . . . if nobody laughs in the middle.
> —BARNEY C. BLACK, Alexandria, Virginia

***Blake's Lament.***  If I'd known I was gonna live this long, I'd have taken better care of myself.
> —Jazzman EUBIE BLAKE on his 100th birthday, February 7, 1983

***Blick's Rule of Life.***  You have two chances, slim and none.
> —UNKNOWN ORIGIN; from J. Patricia Reilly, New York City

***Blount's Law of Bluffing.***  You can never appear to be cleverer than you are if you never fake anything.
> —ROY BLOUNT, JR., quoted in the September 1984 issue of the *Atlantic Monthly;* from Steve Stine

*Boatman's Law.* Common sense is exceeded only by the ability to recognize it.

——EARL BOATMAN, Rockford, Tennessee

*Bokum's Advice.* You can't be happy with a woman who pronounces both *d*'s in *Wednesday*.

——"DOG" BOKUM, a character from Bob Specht's *Expectation of Days,* 1982

*Borstelmann's Rule.* If everything seems to be coming your way, you're probably in the wrong lane.

——UNKNOWN ORIGIN; from Donald R. Woods

*Boucher's Observations.* (1) He who blows his own horn always plays the music several octaves higher than originally written. (2) You can't have the ocean except at sea level.

——SHARON BOUCHER, Placerville, California

*Bowers's Law.* Hubris always boomerangs.

——DR. JOHN BOWERS; from Jo Rozanski, Normal, Illinois

*Boyle's Laws.* (1) There are people you cannot trust with your money; so it is with your emotions. (2) Fate will do everything possible to put you into publicly embarrassing situations. (3) Every life is a solo flight. (4) A child being dressed will insert the opposite limb.

——CHARLES BOYLE, Annapolis, Maryland

*Bradley's Reminder.* Everything comes to him who waits— among other things, death.

> —English writer FRANCIS H. BRADLEY

*Brauer's Warning.* He who tries to pick all the flowers is sure to get some poison ivy.

> —DAVID F. BRAUER, Orlando, Florida

*Brenne's Laws of Life.* (1) You never get it where you want it. (2) If you think it's tough now, just wait.

> —CAROL PIKE, Mesa, Arizona, who heard them from her father
> at least once a week during her formative years. She says,
> "These laws can be applied to anything."

*Brock's Advice.* Always wear well-made, good-fitting, expensive shoes and keep them clean, no matter how poor you are.

> —D. R. BROCK, Dayton, Ohio

*Brodersen's Never-Never Land.* (1) Never shake hands with a man holding a chainsaw. (2) Never try to put on a pullover while eating a caramel apple. (3) Never kiss the hand of a lady after she's been to the self-service gas station. (4) Never try to adjust your clothing in a crowded elevator. (5) Never use a felt-tipped marker to clean your ears. (6) Never ask the highway commissioner if he plays bridge. (7) Never wave to your friends at an auction.

> —WILLIAM E. BRODERSEN, Northfield, Minnesota

*Broome's Discovery.* A good-looking (wo)man will get your attention. A bright (wo)man will hold your attention.
——DAVID BROOME, Phoenix, Arizona

*Brown's Laws.* (1) Any sentence with more than three punctuation marks should be rewritten. (2) If a speaker takes a physical breath because a sentence is too long, the audience will take a mental pause that will break concentration. (Whew!) (3) Anything written to another person is sure to a) end up in someone else's hands, b) be misunderstood, and c) be photocopied. (4) Middle age begins when you start thinking about it, but stop talking about it. (5) You are old when you cite a historical event—and you were there. (6) A memo longer than one page is no longer a memo. (7) Your self-imagined importance is in direct proportion to the illegibility of your signature. (8) I give ulcers; I don't get them. (9) Any newspaper ad for a movie that takes up a full page means it is a loser.
——DAVID H. BROWN, Rockville, Maryland

*Brown's Point.* One of the virtues of propaganda is that it is easy to understand.

*Brown's Revision.* Man does not breed by love alone.

*Brown's Postulate.* No matter how low your own self-esteem, there are probably others who think less of you.

*Brown's Fourth Aphorism.* Nothing worth learning is learned quickly except parachuting.

—PROFESSOR DAVID S. BROWN, Washington, D.C.

*Brozik's Laws About Hitting People.* (1) Never hit anybody bigger than you are because a) it is not a nice thing to do and b) you will get the snot beaten out of you. (2) Never hit anybody the same size as you are because a) it is not a nice thing to do and b) regardless of the outcome you will experience some degree of pain and suffering. (3) Never hit anybody smaller than you are because a) it is not a nice thing to do and b) when you turn around to walk away, the victim will rise up and nail you from behind.

—DALLAS BROZIK, Huntington, West Virginia

*Bryant's Rule.* When a stranger identifies you from a friend's description, it's just as well you didn't hear the description.

—LARRY BRYANT, Alexandria, Virginia; quoted in the Spring
1995 *Phoenix Newsletter*

***Budri's Generalizations.*** (1) People always find the time to do the things they want to do. (2) People always find the money to get the things they want to get.

—VINCENT BUDRI, Longmeadow, Massachusetts

***Bullfrog's Laws of Survival.*** (1) If it's bigger than you, run from it. (2) If it's smaller than you, eat it. (3) If it's the same size, mate with it.

—TONY VECCHIO, director of the Roger Williams Park Zoo; from Barry Nordin, Warwick, Rhode Island

***Byrne's Law of Concreting.*** When you pour, it rains.

—UNKNOWN ORIGIN; from Donald Kaul's column in the *Des Moines Register,* December 11, 1978

***Caldwell's National Constant.*** Americans have more time-saving devices and less time than any other group of people in the world.

—DUNCAN CALDWELL, quoted in *The Bedside Coronet*

***Callum's Advice.*** Find out what you don't do well, then don't do it.

—MYLES CALLUM

***Campbell's Law.*** A sinner can reform, but stupid is forever.

—LT. COL. WILLIAM P. CAMPBELL III, USAF, Eglin Air Force Base, Florida

***Campbell's Law of Criticism.*** When you hear person A criticizing person B, you learn more about person A than about person B.

—JAMES G. CAMPBELL, Toorak, Victoria, Australia

*Canfield's Corollary to the "You Can't Win 'Em All Rule."*
You can't even *fight* 'em all.

—MONTE CANFIELD, formerly of the General Accounting Office; from Sharon Lynn, Washington, D.C.

*Carol's Rule.* Never run after a bus or a man; if you miss one, there will be another along in a few minutes.

—CAROL DENNIS, Chicago, Illinois

*Carville's Challenge.* Here's a quarter; call somebody who gives a damn.

—Clinton political strategist JAMES CARVILLE, quoted on Whitewater, June 1, 1996

*Carvlin's Commentary.* In marriage, a warm heart seldom compensates for cold hands.

—TOM CARVLIN, Dolton, Illinois

*Chesterton's Warning.* Never invoke gods unless you really want them to appear. It annoys them very much.

—G. K. CHESTERTON (1874–1936); from Sarah Risher, Bethesda, Maryland

*C. J.'s Law.* Philosophy doesn't get the washing-up done.

—C. J., a character in the British TV series *The Rise and Fall of Reginald Perrin*; from Shel Kagan

*Claudia's Assurance.* When writing a personal letter, as soon as you begin a new sheet of paper, you will run out of things to say.

—CLAUDIA COSTELLO, Manassas, Virginia

*Clements's Premise.* Assumption and presumption are the parents of all foul-ups.

—E. STALEY CLEMENTS, JR., Christiansburg, Virginia

*Cliff's Catalog of the Least Credible English Quotations.* Of course I'll respect you in the morning.

—UNKNOWN ORIGIN; from Gregg Townsend, Tucson, Arizona

*Clifton's Advice.* Don't give up high ground 'til you know you're over the pass. *Clifton's Conclusion.* Anything designed to do more than one thing does no thing very well. *Corollary.* Don't buy a car that flies.

—KELLY H. CLIFTON, Hiroshima, Japan

*Close's Clever Cue for Clashing Couples.* If I can prove I'm right, I make things worse.

—REV. HENRY CLOSE, Fort Lauderdale, Florida, in Letters to the Editor, *Time,* March 19, 1979

*Clovis's Consideration of an Atmospheric Anomaly.* The perversity of nature is nowhere better demonstrated than by the fact that, when exposed to the same atmosphere, bread becomes hard while crackers become soft.

—E. ROBERT CLOVIS; from Stephen Bishop

*Clyde's Law.* If you have something to do, and you put it off long enough, chances are someone else will do it for you.

—CLYDE F. ADAMS, Auburn, Alabama

*Cohen's Law.* There is no bottom to worse.

—ROBERT V. COHEN, M.D., Abington, Pennsylvania, who learned it from his grandfather

*Comer's Law.* Never mistake asthma for passion and vice versa.

—A. J. COMER, Huntington Valley, Pennsylvania

*Condon's Law of Return.* The size of the car in which a past pupil arrives for the college reunion is in inverse proportion to the size of the brain of that pupil.

—JOHN CONDON, Dublin, Ireland

*Conrad's Rule.* One advantage of old age is that there are more younger women all the time.

—CHARLES CONRAD III, Racine, Wisconsin

*Cooper's Discovery.* Life isn't fair, but neither is death.

—ED COOPER; from Martin Kottmeyer, Carlyle, Illinois

*Cooper's Law for Practicing Politicians.* Principles become modified in practice by facts.

> —Quoted by JAMES J. KILPATRICK in his column, April 3, 1981;
> from Steve Woodbury

*Coper's Complaint.* We could handle all of life's stress if only we could find the handles.

> —UNKNOWN ORIGIN; from Neal Wilgus

*Corcoran's Law of Shrinkage:* Everything from your past seems smaller when you see it again except your old flame. *Corcoran's First Law of Sex Laws.* It is more fun trying to think up sex laws than any other laws.

> —JOHN H. CORCORAN, JR., created while in Washington, D.C.
> He is now a screenwriter in Los Angeles.

*Cosgrave's Law.* People will often sell their friends down the river in order to impress those they do not like.

> —Former Irish Prime Minister LIAM COSGRAVE, who noted that
> the British were known for selling their friends down the river
> to appease their enemies; from Peter Robinson, Paris

*Cotter's Laundromat Mystery.* Why is it that when there's an attendant to make change, the change machine works, and when there isn't, it doesn't?

> —JOHN COTTER, in the *Washington Post,* December 6, 1987

*Cozgriff's First Principle for Dealing with Potentially Life-Threatening Situations.* Relax—otherwise you might die all tensed up.

    —CADET RALPH COZGRIFF; from David Little

*The Cronkites' Contrary Views of Death.* WALTER CRONKITE: "When I go, I'd like to go like Errol Flynn—on the deck of my 70-foot yacht with a 16-year-old mistress." BETTY CRONKITE: "You're going to go on a 16-foot boat with your 70-year-old mistress."

    —In *USA Today*'s compilation of 1986's Unforgettable Quotes

*Crudup's Law.* Mediocrity always succeeds over originality.

    —ANONYMOUS; from Nigel Stapley

***Dale's Dictum.*** People don't make the same mistake twice; they make it three times, four times, or five times.

—MICHAEL DALE

***Daniel's Delight.*** If it is ironic, it is probably true.

—D. PARK TETER, Hazelhurst, Wisconsin

***Dato's Law.*** Wishes expand in direct proportion to the resources available for their gratification.

—ROBERT DATO, Wynnewood, Pennsylvania

***Daugherty's List of Things a Person Should Never Say.*** (1) "That's impossible!" (2) "You can't do that to me!" (3) "I'll love you forever." (4) "And that's my final offer!" (5) "I'll never hurt you." (6) "This hurts me more than it hurts you." (7) "It'll be a cold day in hell before I'll ever do that!"

—WILLIAM J. DAUGHERTY

*David's Law of Habits.* Any bad habit is easier than the corresponding good habit.

— DAVID MCKAY, Havertown, Pennsylvania

*Davidson's Law of Weather Variance.* The arrival of spring always trails expectations. The arrival of summer always precedes expectations. Autumn arrives on time. Winter arrives when it wants to.

— JEFF DAVIDSON, Falls Church, Virginia

*Davis's Dictum.* Problems that go away by themselves come back by themselves.

— MARCY E. DAVIS, Philadelphia, Pennsylvania

*DeCaprio's Rule.* Everything takes more time and money.

— ANNIE DECAPRIO, High Bridge, New Jersey

*DeRock's Law of Dullness.* Dullness is directly proportional to the number of brown suits in a crowd.

— DOUG DEROCK, Western Springs, Illinois

*Dickson's Definition.* A pessimist is a person who mourns the future.

— The late ISABELLE C. DICKSON, the Director's mother, formerly of Hastings-on-Hudson, New York, and Yonkers, New York

*Dmitri's Epigrams.* (1) Nobody can ever get too much approval. (2) No matter how much you want or need, *they,* whoever *they* are, don't want to let you get away with it, whatever *it* is. (3) Sometimes you get away with it.

> —JOHN LEONARD, who sometimes called himself Dmitri in his *New York Times* columns; from his column

*Doc Scoggins's Reminder.* You're only young once, but you can be immature all your life.

> —CHARLES SCOGGINS, M.D., quoted in the June 1981 *Internist,* in reference to his avocation as a member of a rodeo roping team; from Bernard Albert

*Doris's Law of Looks.* No matter what you wear, you will not look good if you look cold.

> —DORIS BROWN, Glen Ellyn, Illinois

*Dorothea's Comforting Thought for the Day.* I've broken so many mirrors in my life, if I live long enough to have all that bad luck, I'll be lucky.

> —DOROTHEA GILDAR, Washington, D.C.

*Dottie's Law.* Any attempt to simplify creates more complications.

> —DOROTHY TURCOTTE, Grimsby, Ontario, Canada

*Douskey's Rule Concerning the Odds of Capitalizing on Previous Success.* Sequels never equal.

> —FRANZ DOUSKEY, Mount Carmel, Connecticut

*Dr. Hayes's Hint.* Helpful hints aren't.

—BRIAN E. HAYES, M.D., Rosebud, Oregon

*Dr. J's Distinction.*
*If they say they love you,*
*trust their behavior. If they say they don't love you,*
*trust their words.*

—JOHN H. DICKEY, PH.D., Aurora, Colorado

*Dude's Law of Duality.*  Of two possible events, only the undesired one will occur.

This can be expressed mathematically as:

$$A^u \vee B \rightarrow A \ [1]$$
$$A \vee B^u \rightarrow B \ [2]$$

where A and B are possible outcomes, the superscript $^u$ denotes the
undesired outcome, and $\vee$ means either/or.

—From WALTER MULÉ's article, "Beyond Murphy's Law," in
*Northliner.* Mulé says the law was named for Sam Dude, whose
genius was cut short by a skydiving accident that occurred just
after he was forced to choose between two types of parachute.

*Dunlop's Determination.*  People complain most about that
over which they have the least control—i.e., the weather.

—PAUL DUNLOP, Hamilton, Ontario

***Ehrman's Corollary to Ginsberg's Theorem.*** (1) Things will get worse before they get better. (2) Who said things would get better?

— JOHN EHRMAN, Stanford Linear Accelerator Center, California

***Electronic Elegy.*** Beware of buying anything when the manuals are bigger than the equipment.

— B. V. D. SMITH, Downers Grove, Illinois

***Eliot's Observation.*** Nothing is so good as it seems beforehand.

— GEORGE ELIOT

***Ellison's Conclusion.*** The two most common things in the universe are hydrogen and stupidity.

— HARLAN ELLISON in *Omni* magazine, February 1987; spotted by Catherine Pfeifer

*Elsner's Observations.* (1) Calories are delicious. (2) Smokers cannot read. (3) Humor is dependent on the truth.

—RAYMOND F. ELSNER, Littleton, Colorado

*Emerson's Insight.* That which we call sin in others is experiment for us.

—RALPH WALDO EMERSON

*Ertz's Observation on Immortality.* Millions long for immortality who do not know what to do with themselves on a rainy Sunday afternoon.

—SUSAN ERTZ

*e-Rules, e-Observations, and Assorted e-Truths Encountered Online.* (1) Once I thought I was wrong, but I was mistaken. (2) The colder the X-ray table, the more of your body is required on it. (3) The severity of the itch is inversely proportional to the ease with which it is reached. (4) Life can only be understood backwards, but it must be lived forwards. (5) Give a man a fish and he will eat for a day. Teach him how to fish, and he will sit in a boat and drink beer all day.

—UNKNOWN ORIGIN; from the Internet

*Eternal Questions from Cyberspace.* (1) If the number 2 pencil is the most popular, why is it still number 2? (2) If all the world is a stage, where is the audience sitting? (3) If you try to fail, and succeed, which have you done?

> —UNKNOWN ORIGIN; from the Internet

*Ettorre's Observation.* The other line moves faster.

> —BARBARA ETTORRE, New York City. This law first appeared in
> *Harper's* in August 1974, and it has become a bona fide hit,
> showing up on almost every list of laws produced since then.
> It was originally published in a longer version, to wit: "The
> other line moves faster. This applies to all lines—bank, super-
> market, tollbooth, customs, and so on. And don't try to
> change lines. The other line—the one you were in originally—
> will then move faster."

*Evelyn's Law.* A woman is like a tea bag—you never know her strength until she gets into hot water.

> —EVELYN, a woman who phoned a radio call-in show, WRC,
> Washington, D.C.

*"Ever Notice" Observation.* Ever notice that even the busiest people are never too busy to tell you just how busy they are?

> —UNKNOWN ORIGIN; overheard on the subway in
> Washington, D.C.

*The Exploding Water Heater Theory.* You should live every day as if tomorrow you were going to be killed by an exploding water heater.

> —JEREMY EHRLICH, San Francisco, California, who explains, "The background for this theory has to do with the following observations: Dentists tend to have clean teeth, for dentists understand the importance of brushing. Chiropractors have good posture, for they understand the importance of a healthy back. Firefighters remember to replace the batteries in their fire alarms, etc. Consider Hypothetical Joe, who tries to do all of this. He brushes his teeth, works out, replaces his batteries, the whole bit. One day he's in the basement working on some repair around the house when he is killed because he has forgotten to replace his water heater every five to seven years like he was supposed to."

*Eyberg's Romantic Reminder.* Regardless of how good we are *in* bed, our relationship is entirely dependent on how good we are *out* of bed.

> —JOHN E. EYBERG, Columbia, Missouri

**Farmer's Law.** The easiest crops to grow are weeds and pests.
—Heard at the University of California, Davis; from Tom Gill

**Fitz-Gibbon's Law.** Creativity varies inversely with the number of cooks involved with the broth.
—BERNICE FITZ-GIBBON in *Macy's, Gimbels, and Me*

**Forbes's Rule.** You have to work quickly and find a niche.
—THE DIRECTOR; from *Forbes,* October 6, 1986

**The Fox Epiphenomenon.** If you do nothing, nothing will happen. If you do something, something will happen—but not what you intended.
—JAMES F. FOX, New York City

*Frankenfeld's Revised Proverbs.* (1) It is better to have loved and had delirious sex than to have loved and lost. (2) All's war in love and fairness. (3) Before having a midlife crisis, it is usually best to have a life. (4) It is difficult to take any group seriously that actually uses the term "tanning consultant." (5) A watched pot is usually owned by someone without cable. (6) I came. I saw. I refinanced.
> —PHILIP J. FRANKENFELD, Chicago, Illinois

*Fraraccio's Law.* It's not *what* you know, it's how fast you can find it out.
> —JOHN C. FRARACCIO, Brick Town, New Jersey

*Fraser's Additions.* Love is like snow: you don't know when it will come or how long it will last or how much you'll get.
> —ALEX FRASER, Washington, D.C.

*Frensham's Maxim of Constructive Apathy.* For every reason there is for doing something, there are at least three for not doing it (you just have to find them all).
> —RAY FRENSHAM, Barkingside, Essex, U.K., who practices constructive apathy, or "the science of life passing you by."

*Fuchs's Fact.* If your name can be spelled wrong, it will be.
> —MONIKA FUCHS, Stockholm, Sweden

*Fullner's Rules.* (1) *Public Telephones.* A public telephone is never being used except when you want to use it. (2) *Bad Examples.* A bad example is more readily followed than a good one.

        —RANDALL L. FULLNER, San Jose, California

*Gage's Rule.* Integrity is like oxygen—the higher you go, the less there is of it.

—PETE GAGE, Pasadena, Texas

*Gamson's Geriatric Corollary to Newton's Laws of Gravity.* Objects fall to earth at a frequency inversely related to the ability of the dropper to pick them up.

—ART GAMSON, Chevy Chase, Maryland

*Gandhi's Observation.* There is more to life than increasing its speed.

—MAHATMA GANDHI

*Gardner's Discovery.* The two greatest things in the world are women and cellophane tape.

—MARTIN GARDNER, Hendersonville, North Carolina

*Gardner's Rule of Society.* The society which scorns excellence in plumbing because plumbing is a humble activity and tolerates shoddiness in philosophy because it is an exalted activity will have neither good plumbing nor good philosophy. Neither its pipes nor its theories will hold water.

—JOHN W. GARDNER, *Forbes,* August 1, 1977

*Geanangel's Law.* If you want to make an enemy, do someone a favor.

—CHARLES L. GEANANGEL, Winter Haven, Florida

*Gerrold's Laws of Infernal Dynamics.* (1) An object in motion will always be headed in the wrong direction. (2) An object at rest will always be in the wrong place. (3) The energy required to change either one of these states will always be more than you wish to expend, but never so much as to make the task totally impossible.

—DAVID GERROLD, writer and columnist for *Starlog* magazine

*Gibson's Bermuda Law.* If the grass is greener on the other side of the fence, your neighbor has an elephant for a pet.

—RON GIBSON, Germantown, Tennessee

*Gillette's Principle.* If you want to make people angry, lie. If you want to make them absolutely livid with rage, tell the truth.

—ROBERT D. GILLETTE, M.D., director of the Riverside Family
Practice Center, Toledo, Ohio

*Glasow's Law.* There's something wrong if you're always right.

—ARNOLD GLASOW, *Forbes,* March 15, 1977

*Godin's Law of the Sexual Revolution.* Sex is here to stay, but it will never be the same.

—GUY GODIN, Université Laval, Quebec, from his unpublished paper *The Five or Six Ages of Sex*

*Gold's Law.* There are two four-letter sources for 90 percent of all human troubles: S-E-X-X and M-U-N-Y.

—HERBERT RESNICOW, *The Gold Solution;* from Charles D. Poe

*Gooden's Rule.* A woman's opinion of a man's sexual attraction is always in inverse ratio to her own sexual attraction.

—B. B. W. GOODEN, Twickenham, Middlesex, England

*Goodfader's Law.* Under any system a few sharpies will beat the rest of us.

—AL GOODFADER, Washington, D.C.

*Grant's Idea of Hell.* Hell is where you go after you die, and all the ideas you ever forgot come back to you.

—MICHAEL GRANT, in the *San Diego Union,* San Diego, California

*Great American Axiom.* Some is good; more is better. Too much is just right.

—UNKNOWN ORIGIN; collected on a radio call-in show

*Greene's Law.* Life is a do-it-yourself project.

—BILL GREENE; from Joseph M. McCabe, Martinsburg, West Virginia

*Grizzard's Discovery.* Regardless of what you might accomplish in life, the size of your funeral is still going to be determined by the weather.

—The late LOUIS GRIZZARD

*Groucho's Point.* If women dressed for men, the stores wouldn't sell much. Just an occasional sun visor.

—GROUCHO MARX on *You Bet Your Life*

*Gumperson's Law.* The probability of anything happening is in inverse ratio to its desirability.

—This very important law first appeared in the November 1957 issue of *Changing Times* and was credited to Dr. R. F. Gumperson. The law was announced in conjunction with a long-forgotten article on firewood, to account for a phenomenon known to anyone who has ever lit fires, to wit: ". . . that you can throw a burnt match out the window of your car and start a forest fire while you can use two boxes of matches and a whole edition of the Sunday paper without being able to start a fire under the dry logs in your fireplace."

Gumperson began serious work in 1938 on the *Farmers' Almanac* phenomenon (by which that esteemed annual always does a better job predicting the weather than the official weather bureau) and during World War II went on to develop the procedure for the armed forces " . . . whereby the more a recruit knew about a given subject, the better chance he had of receiving an assignment involving some other subject."

Some of the many real-life examples he was able to derive from his law and his pioneering work as a divicist: *

The person who buys the most raffle tickets has the least chance of winning.

Good parking places are always on the other side of the street.

It was further reported that Gumperson met with an untimely death in 1947 while walking down the highway. He was obeying the proper rule of walking on the left facing traffic when he was hit from behind by a Hillman-Minx driven by an Englishman hugging the left.

Over the years Gumperson has picked up many disciples, including the late H. Allen Smith, who wrote that he felt that the law was written just for him. One of Smith's many examples: "I dislike going to the garage with a rattle in my car, because the moment the mechanic begins his inspection, that rattle will vanish."

*One skilled in divicism. Divicism is the science of making predictions according to the law of diverges. A diverge is the opposite of an average.

**Gumperson's Proof.** The most undesirable things are the most certain (e.g., death and taxes).

—EDWIN GUTHMAN; from Mark B. Cohen's collected "Laws of Politics"

**Gustafson's Observation.** There is no virtue in consistency if you are consistently wrong.

—ART GUSTAFSON; from Lloyd W. Vanderman, Oxon Hill, Maryland

**Gwinn's Theory of Necessity.** Whenever you need it, it's never there; but if you don't need it, it's everywhere. *Ergo:* It's always in your face except when needed.

—MARCEL GWINN, Houston, Texas

*Haas's Universal Truth.* Everybody's holidays are a nuisance, except one's own.

—TIMOTHY HAAS, Woldingham, Surrey, U.K.

*Hagemann's Five Principles of the Common Law.* (1) People are no damn good. (2) Creditors always win. (3) Avoid litigation. (4) It isn't the principle of the thing, it's the money. (5) The undertaker is always paid first.

—JOHN HAGEMANN, Vermillion, South Dakota

*Hakala's Rule of Survival.* Pack your own parachute.

—T. L. HAKALA, Mesa, Arizona

*Hallen's Credo.*
If you bend like the willow, you will never break your back—
but you may find your nose on the ground.
—WALTER SCOTT HALLEN, Evanston, Illinois

*Harrel's Collection of "Worst Questions I Have Been Asked."*
(1) Where did you lose it? (2) Have I kept you waiting? (3) You
asleep? (4) Will you promise not to get mad if I ask you something?
(5) You don't remember me, do you?

*Harrel's Discoveries.* (1) When a part of your anatomy is hurt-
ing, every friend you meet will hit you in that spot. (2) You can
always judge a man's character by his activities when he is away
from home.
—C. JACK HARREL, Kingfisher, Oklahoma

*Hartig's "How Is Good Old Bill?" "We're Divorced" Law.*
If there is a wrong thing to say, one will. *Hartig's "Sleeve in the Cup,
Thumb in the Butter" Law.* When one is trying to be elegant and
sophisticated, one won't be.
—BETTY HARTIG, "the Nantucket Kitelady," Nantucket,
Massachusetts

*Hasselbring's Law.* Never remember what you can afford to
forget.
—ANDREW S. HASSELBRING, Chillicothe, Ohio

*Haviland's Discoveries.* (1) *Law of Thermodynamics.* Hot hand air dryers in public washrooms will shut off just as they reach a sufficient temperature to actually begin the drying process and will always have to be restarted. You will never need the full time on the second cycle. (2) *Time's Truth.* You do not necessarily have to be having fun for time to fly. (3) *Dieter's Despair.* There are more food commercials on TV when you are on a diet.

—JAMES D. HAVILAND, Halifax, Nova Scotia

*Hazlitt's Conjecture on Consistency.* Never say "never" and always avoid "always." *Hazlitt's Observation.* The right thing to say always comes to mind after you've said the wrong thing and have no opportunity for rebuttal.

—JOHN M. HAZLITT, South Bend, Indiana

*Healy's Law of Distance.* The promised land always looks better from a distance.

—PAT HEALY, reporter, the *Boston Globe*

*Hein's Law.* Problems worthy of attack prove their worth by hitting back.

—PIET HEIN, from a group of "Quips" in *Journal of Irreproducible Results*, March 1971

*Hellmann's Principle.* Keep cool but do not freeze.

—A. PETER HOLLIS, Wilson, North Carolina

*Herblock's Law.* If it's good, they'll stop making it.

—Conceived by HERBERT BLOCK, the famous political cartoonist, after they stopped making a particular kind of carbon drawing stick that he liked best. Reported on by Sydney J. Harris in his December 28, 1977, syndicated column, "Modern Way: If It's Good, Scrap It."

*Herth's Law.* He who turns the other cheek too far gets it in the neck.

—UNKNOWN ORIGIN; from a caller to a radio call-in show

*Hinson's Discoveries.* Never, never read the fine print. There ain't no way you're gonna like it. . . . Otherwise, it would be printed in large print.

—ARCHIE EDWARD HINSON, El Cajon, California

*Horton's Law.* For difficult Yes/No decisions (especially regarding the opposite sex) you'll always wish you did if you didn't, but you'll rarely wish you didn't if you did.

> —JOSEPH A. HORTON, M.D., Philadelphia, who adds that this is also known as "The Ah Posteriori Law."

*Horton's Maxims.* (1) Nature always wins. (2) Nothing is waterproof.

> —SCOTT HORTON, San Francisco, California

*Hovancik's "Wait till Tomorrow" Principle.* Today is the last day of the first part of your life.

> —JOHN HOVANCIK, South Orange, New Jersey

*Hoyle's Hoylerism.* Good enough isn't.

> —BETTY HOYLE, Orlando, Florida

*Huhn's Law.* You're not late until you get there.

> —UNKNOWN ORIGIN; from a radio call-in show

*Hull's Warning.* Never insult an alligator until after you have crossed the river.

> —Former Secretary of State CORDELL HULL

*Hungarian Proverb.* Life is like a baby's diaper—short and messy.

> —UNKNOWN ORIGIN; collected on a radio call-in show, Washington, D.C.

*Hutzler's Refutation.* Desperation, not necessity, is the mother of invention.

> —THOMAS L. HUTZLER, Technical Sgt., USAF, Fort Fisher, North Carolina

*Hynes's Advice.* When you have a lot of things to do, get your nap out of the way first.

> —JEREMIAH HYNES; from his daughter, Jo Anderson, Deerfield, Illinois

*Igbara's Equation.* If there are two events of equal importance they will always conflict (e.g., marriage and career).

　　—NEEKA IGBARA, Port Harcourt, Nigeria

*Inertia, Law of.* Given enough time, what you put off doing today will eventually get done by itself.

　　—G. GESTRA, Oregon

*Inskip's Rules.* (1) Don't sweat the small stuff. (2) It's all small stuff.

　　—DR. RICHARD INSKIP, director of the American Academy of
　　　Family Physicians. This set of rules has also been attributed to
　　　University of Nebraska cardiologist ROBERT ELIOT.

*Issawi on Sex and Money.* Sex and money are like tea and coffee—two delicious ingredients which, when mixed together, produce a foul concoction.

—CHARLES ISSAWI, Princeton, New Jersey

***Jacobson's Law of Matchmaking.*** If you try to sneak your way through a surprise introduction of a co-worker to your best college friend, you will quickly learn they were divorced from one another in 1982.

      —ROBERTA B. JACOBSON, APO, New York

***Jacoby's Law.*** The more intelligent and competent a woman is in her adult life, the less likely she is to have received an adequate amount of romantic attention in adolescence.

      —SUSAN JACOBY in the *New York Times.* "If a girl was smart," she goes on to explain, "and if she attended an American high school between 1930 and 1965, chances are that no one paid attention to anything but her brains unless she took the utmost care to conceal them."

*James's Distinction.* "Intelligent" is a term used for someone who agrees with you. "Brilliant" means that you agree with him, but would never have thought of the idea yourself.

—Baseball writer and analyst BILL JAMES from his *1983 Baseball Abstract*

*January's Cruel Lesson.* You will not win one of those million-dollar magazine sweepstakes that come in the mail. Knowing this, you will spend hours filling them out and in the process will accidentally order a magazine devoted to either subsistence farming, needlepoint, or bow hunting.

—THE DIRECTOR

*Jean's Law.* Keep your feet close to the ground.

—JEAN PIKE, Modesto, California

*Jefferson's Ten Commandments.* (1) Never put off till tomorrow what you can do today. (2) Never trouble another for what you can do yourself. (3) Never spend your money before you have earned it. (4) Never buy what you don't want because it is cheap. (5) Pride costs more than hunger, thirst, and cold. (6) We seldom report of having eaten too little. (7) Nothing is troublesome that we do willingly. (8) How much pain evils cost us that have never happened! (9) Take things always by the smooth handle. (10) When angry, count to ten before you speak; if very angry, count to a 100.

—THOMAS JEFFERSON; found in *Thoughts on the Business Life,* edited by B. C. Forbes

*Jennifer's Law.* The more truth there is in what a woman is saying, the less a man is listening.

—JENNIFER FEENSTRA, Montreal, Quebec, Canada

*Jensen's Law.* When you're hot, you're hot, and when you're not, everybody is watching.

—LYNN JENSEN, Littleton, Colorado

*Judy's Questions.* Does it really matter? What if it did?

—Sign posted outside the office of JUDY KLINDT; submitted by co-worker Carol Dennis of Chicago, Illinois

*Jump's Discovery.* Life is a lot like golf: you drive hard to get to the green and then you end up in the hole.

—GARY JUMP, Bensenville, Illinois

***Keil's Warning.*** In becoming sly as a fox, you will catch fleas.

—PETER A. KEIL, St. Louis, Missouri

***Kelly's Credos.*** (1) The older you get, the greater the difference between the age you look and the age you think you look. (2) The ability to take off a pair of tight jeans while standing up without holding onto anything correlates positively with your ability to enjoy whatever activity follows their removal. (3) If at any gathering of twelve or more persons you say something nasty about an absent person, a friend or relative of that person will be present.

—MARY EVALYN OWEN KELLY, Kansas City, Missouri, who sent these in a 1995 note with this P.S.: "My birth certificate says that I am 77, but I'm pretty sure there's some mistake."

*Kidd's Enlightenment.* Things aren't like they used to be, and they never were.
—TED KIDD, Traverse City, Michigan

*Kiesel's Railroading Analogy.* You often find that one-track minds are narrow-gauge as well.
—GEORGE F. KIESEL, St. Louis, Missouri

*Kime's Law for the Reward of Meekness.* Turning the other cheek merely ensures two bruised cheeks.
—JACK KIME, Las Cruces, New Mexico

*Kinsley's Law.* Insincere flattery is even more flattering than sincere flattery. *Corollary.* All flattery is flattering.
—MICHAEL KINSLEY, in the *New Republic,* January 20, 1985

*Kipling's Comparison.* There's worser things than marching from Oombalah to Cawnpore.
—RUDYARD KIPLING (1837–1911), from his poem
"*Route Marching*"; from Georgia Bender

*Koppel's Credo with Definition.* The optimist believes in the triumph of hope over expectations, my favorite definition of which is an accordion player with a beeper.
—TED KOPPEL in a commencement address at
Tufts University, 1994

*Kozub's Laws.* (1) Home-grown ice (in your freezer) is never clear. (2) Super glue isn't. (3) Tab A rarely fits Slot A. (4) Absence makes the heart go wander.

—FRED KOZUB, Richmond, Virginia

*Kraft's Admonition.* Do it now—otherwise, by the time you get around to it, it will be too late.

—BARBARA S. KRAFT, Washington, D.C.

*Lamb's Law.* The world meets nobody halfway.

    —CHARLES LAMB (1775–1834)

*Landers's Revision.* The best things in life aren't things.

    —ANN LANDERS in *Forbes FYI*

*Larson's Conclusion.* Shunning women, liquor, gambling, smoking, and eating will not make one live longer. It will only seem like it.

    —MASTER SGT., ROBERT V. LARSON, USAF (retired), Golden
    Valley, Minnesota

*Leahy's Law.* If a thing is done wrong often enough, it becomes right. *Corollary.* Volume is a defense against error.

    —RICHARD A. LEAHY, Boston, Massachusetts

*Liebling's Law.*  If you just try long enough and hard enough, you can always manage to boot yourself in the posterior.
>  —A. J. LIEBLING, in *The Press*

*Lindsey's Law of Youth.*  The youth are always worse than the preceding generation were, in the opinion of the latter.
>  —In JUSTICE BEN B. LINDSEY's *Revolt of Modern Youth*; from
>  Leon M. Louw

*Lin's Maxim.*  Happiness is a state of minimum regret.
>  —WALLACE E. LIN, Hartford, Connecticut

*Linus's Law.*  There is no heavier burden than great potential.
>  —LINUS, a character from Charles M. Schulz's comic strip
>  *Peanuts;* from Gerald M. Fava, Lake Hiawatha, New Jersey

*Lloyd's Laws of Autopsy.*  (1) Always make sure you're doing the autopsy on the right body. (2) Always make sure the patient is dead.
>  —Pathologist HUMPHREY LLOYD of Beverly, Massachusetts;
>  collected by Bob Skole

*Longworth's Philosophy.*  Fill what's empty. Empty what's full. And scratch where it itches.
>  —ALICE ROOSEVELT LONGWORTH (1884–1980)

*The Lopez Law of Life.* Never be without a book. The day you forget to bring a book is the day you will get stuck in an elevator (traffic jam, etc.) for two hours and forty-five minutes.

—MARSHA LOPEZ, Westmont, Illinois

*Lowell's Constant.* Whatever you may be sure of, be sure of this: that you are dreadfully like other people.

—JAMES RUSSELL LOWELL (1819–1891); quoted in *Catchwords of Worldly Wisdom*

*Lowell's Law of Life.* Life is a hypothesis.

—Poet ROBERT LOWELL (1917–1977)

*Lowrey's Law.* If it jams . . . force it. If it breaks, it needed replacing anyway.

—UNKNOWN ORIGIN

*Lowrey's Law of Expertise.* Just when you get really good at something, you don't need to do it anymore.

—WILLIAM P. LOWREY, Sidney, Illinois

*Luce's Law.* No good deed goes unpublished.

—CLARE BOOTHE LUCE

*Lucy's Law.* The alternative to getting old is depressing.

—UNKNOWN ORIGIN; from Donald R. Woods

***Mame's Lament.*** Life is a banquet, and most damned fools are starving to death.

—AUNTIE MAME, a character in the play of the same name

***Marquis's Revised Maxim.*** Every cloud has its silver lining, but it is sometimes a little difficult to get it to the mint. ***Marquis's Understanding.*** Middle age is the time when a man is always thinking that in a week or two he will feel as good as ever.

—Humorist DON MARQUIS

***Mary's Rule.*** All men/women have ten faults. Pick ten faults you can live with.

—MARY WILLIAMS; from her son Jon, South Melbourne,
Australia.

*Maugham's Advice.* Death is a very dull, dreary affair, and my advice to you is to have nothing whatsoever to do with it.

—W. SOMERSET MAUGHAM; from Donald R. Woods

*McCarthy's Realization.* If I had my life to live over I'd probably make the same mistakes—only I'd make them sooner.

—CHARLIE MCCARTHY, ventriloquist Edgar Bergen's star dummy, on their radio show

*McCormick's Conclusion.* You're either too young or old enough to know better, but you're never the right age.

—PEGGY MCCORMICK, San Mateo, California

*McDougal's Law.* Planning never beat dumb luck.

—UNKNOWN ORIGIN; from Howard Hamer, Long Branch, New Jersey

*McGoorty's Warning.* One of the worst things that can happen in life is to win a bet on a horse at an early age.

—DANNY MCGOORTY; quoted in *The 637 Best Things Anyone Ever Said,* by Robert Byrne

*McLaren's Motto.* Sic Transit Gloria Tuesday!

—JACK MCLAREN, from *Columbo's Little Book of Canadian Proverbs, Graffiti, Limericks, and Other Vital Matters* by John Robert Columbo

*McNulty's Law.* Never dive in a bikini.
—UNKNOWN ORIGIN; Jeffrey Chamberlain, Nassau, New York

*Meier's Law.* People are like electricity—they take the path of least resistance.
—LEROY W. MEIER, Mt. Healthy, Ohio

*Mel's Law.* If it wasn't for the last minute, nothing would get done.
—UNKNOWN ORIGIN; radio call-in show, New York City

*Mencken's Meta-law.* For every human problem, there is a neat, plain solution—and it is always wrong.
—H. L. MENCKEN

*Merrill's First Corollary.* There are no winners in life; only survivors.
—UNKNOWN ORIGIN

*Metzger's Maxim.* You're only as old as you feel—the next day.
—DANIEL J. METZGER, Belleville, Illinois

*Meuse's Law.* Anything with teeth sooner or later bites.
—JIM MEUSE, Huntington Beach, California

*Meyer's Law of Human Relations.* In all emotional conflicts the thing you find hardest to do is the one thing you should do.
> —MEYER MEYER in John D. MacDonald's *Pale Gray for Guilt;* from Stephen M. Lonsdale, Abington, Massachusetts

*Midas's Law.* Possession diminishes perception of value, immediately.
> —JOHN UPDIKE, in the *New Yorker,* November 3, 1975

*Miller's Law.* You can't tell how deep a puddle is until you step into it.
> —UNKNOWN ORIGIN

*Miller's Principle.* Abstinence makes the heart grow fonder.
> —MARK R. MILLER; from Andrea Miller

*Mintz's Law.* The best things in life are messy.
> —ANN EMMONS MINTZ, Philadelphia, Pennsylvania

*Mitchell's Reminder.* All anybody needs to know about prizes is that Mozart never won one.
> —The late HENRY MITCHELL in the *Washington Post*

*Miz Beaver's Summation of Walt Kelly's Philosophy.* He allus said, don't take life too serious . . . it ain't nohow permanent.

> —MIZ BEAVER, a character in the *Pogo* comic strip, the Christmas following Walt Kelly's death

*Montagu's Maxim.* The idea is to die young as late as possible.

> —Anthropologist ASHLEY MONTAGU

*Moos's Law.* When it is necessary to choose between ignorance and stupidity, choose ignorance. It is curable.

> —PHIL MOOS, M.D., St. Cloud, Minnesota

*Morley's Conclusion.* No man is lonely while eating spaghetti.

> —Actor ROBERT MORLEY (1908–1992)

*Mother Sigafoo's Observation.* A man should be greater than some of his parts.

> —Uttered by MOTHER SIGAFOO in Peter DeVries's *I Hear America Swinging*

*The Murphy Validity Proof.* If it's funny, it must be true.

> —SIDNEY I. RISKIN, Tarrytown, New York

*Murray's Law.* If everything else fails, throw it away.

> —JIM MURRAY; from his *Los Angeles Times* column of November 23, 1978

*Murray's Probability.* If you have a 50 percent chance of being right, 90 percent of the time you are wrong. *Proofs:* (1) When trying to decide if the word is spelled "ie" or "ei," I'm wrong 90 percent of the time. (2) There are two lines at the post office, the bank tellers' windows, or the toll gates, and you pick the slow one 90 percent of the time.

—ROBERT H. MURRAY, Wescosville, Pennsylvania

*Napier's Completeness Law.* The absolute conviction that a task has been completed is a good indication that part of it remains to be done.

> —THOMAS M. NAPIER, West Lothian, Scotland, who discovered the law "as a consequence of throwing out the washing-up water before finding more dishes to wash."

*Nathan's Knowledge.* There is never a day so bad that tomorrow couldn't be worse.

> —HARRIET NATHAN, Chicago, Illinois

*Navy Law.* If you can keep your head when all about you others are losing theirs, maybe you just don't understand the situation.

> —Traditional sign that has been showing up on ships and offices of the U.S. Navy for years. It is found elsewhere, too, but is primarily associated with the Navy.

*Nestor's Law.* Anything worth doing makes a mess.

—SIBYL W. NESTOR; from Bonnie Nestor Johnson, Oak Ridge, Tennessee

*Neudel's Law.* The spouse who snores always falls asleep first.

—MARIAN HENRIQUEZ NEUDEL, Chicago, Illinois

*Neuhaus's Rule.* If you like a girl, her boyfriend is *always* a jerk.

—ROBERT NEUHAUS, Chicago, Illinois

*Nevers.* (1) Never eat prunes if you're famished. —UNKNOWN ORIGIN (2) Never play poker with a man whose nickname is a city. —STEWART WOLPIN, quoted in the November 1991 issue of *Vital Speeches* (3) Never, ever mess with the Ladies' Auxiliary. —ANDY GRIFFITH, in his TV show (4) Never buy a portable TV set on the sidewalk from a man who's out of breath. —JOSEPH C. GOULDEN (5) Never trust a man with a tattoo on his face. (6) Never go to a dentist who has teeth painted on his lips. —from the *B.C.* comic strip (7) Never start a project until you've picked out someone to blame. (8) Never buy real estate from a man who works out of a tent. —from *The Wizard of Id* comic strip

*Newchy's Law of Observation.* The probability of being observed is in direct proportion to the stupidity of your actions.

—NEWCHY MIGNONE, Las Vegas, Nevada

*Newman's Discovery.* Your best dreams may not come true; fortunately, neither will your worst dreams.
> —R. A. NEWMAN, Cherry Hill, New Jersey

*Newman's Law.* Hypocrisy is the Vaseline of social intercourse.
> —UNKNOWN ORIGIN; from Roger Newell, Webster, New York

*Norris's Distinction.* Garlic breath is only a problem for other people.
> —BOB NORRIS, Palma Mallorca, Spain

*Norvell's Reminder.* If you would be remembered, do *one* thing superbly well.
> —SAUNDERS NORVELL; from M. Mack Earle, Baltimore,
> Maryland

*Nutter's Dictum.* Good judgment comes from experience, and experience comes from bad judgment.
> —Economist G. WARREN NUTTER; quoted by Walter B. Wriston
> in the *New York Times,* November 4, 1983

**Old Boy's Law.**  You don't learn anything the second time you're kicked by a mule.

  —UNKNOWN ORIGIN; from a radio call-in show

**Orben's Query.**  If sex is such good medicine, how come everybody always needs a refill?

  —BOB ORBEN, Falls Church, Virginia

**O'Shee's Observation.**  It always works better in the commercial.

  —J. P. O'SHEE, Ville Platte, Louisiana

***Ozmon's Laws.*** (1) If someone says they will do something *without fail,* they won't. (2) The more people talk on the phone, the less money they make. (3) People that go to conferences are the ones that shouldn't. (4) Pizza always burns the roof of your mouth.

—HOWARD OZMON, Richmond, Virginia

*Paige's Six Rules for Life (Guaranteed to Bring Anyone to a Happy Old Age).* (1) Avoid fried foods which angry up the blood. (2) If your stomach disputes you, pacify it with cool thoughts. (3) Keep the juices flowing by jangling around gently as you move. (4) Go very lightly on the vices, such as carrying on in society, as the social ramble ain't restful. (5) Avoid running at all times. (6) Don't look back; something might be gaining on you.
—Baseball immortal SATCHEL PAIGE

*Pandora's Rule.* Never open a box you didn't close.
—MIKE BERMAN

*Paper's Law.* The older you get, the more like yourself you got.
—HERBERT H. PAPER, Hebrew Union College, Cincinnati, Ohio

*Paradox of Selective Equality.* All things being equal, all things are never equal.

—MARSHALL L. SMITH, Rockville, Maryland


*Pardo's Postulates.* (1) Anything good is either illegal, immoral, or fattening. (2) The three most faithful things in life are money, a dog, and an old woman. (3) Don't care if you're rich or not, as long as you can live comfortably and have everything you want.

—UNKNOWN ORIGIN; from a collection assembled originally by
Conrad Schneiker, Gregg Townsend, and Ed Logg at the
University of Arizona


*Parsons's Honesty Rule.* If someone replies to your question, "Well, to be honest . . . ," you are entitled to assume that up to that moment he has been telling the most appalling lies. *Parsons's Rule for Collectors.* An essential factor in collecting anything at all is to start twenty years ago.

—DENYS PARSONS, London, England


*Payne's Observation.* There is no man so low that some woman won't want him.

—MABEL PAYNE, Indianapolis, Indiana

*Pea Soup Anderson Law.* We do pea soup well and we make the most out of that.

—RAY BEITEZ, of Pea Soup Anderson's Restaurant, Buellton, California, quoted by Jim Sullivan in *Service That Sells Newsletter*

*Peck's Laws.* (1) Experience is the ability to recognize the same mistake when you make it again. (2) "That won't hold water" is probably what everyone said to the man who invented the sieve. (3) The tremendous advantage of being paranoid is that everything fits. (4) Creative cynicism is the only mortar that can bind rock-headed optimism into the cement of civilization.

—EDWARD L. PECK, Chevy Chase, Maryland

*Pep's Denial of a Report of His Death.* I wasn't even out of the house.

—Former featherweight champion WILLIE PEP, quoted in the *Sporting News* on July 12, 1975

*Petersen's Postulate.* Any sentence beginning with "Ironically" will not contain an irony.

—CLARENCE PETERSEN, the *Chicago Tribune.*

*Peters's Principle of Success.*  Get up one time more than you're knocked down.

> —Country singer JIMMIE PETERS, quoted in the *San Antonio Express News* on January 19, 1979

*Peters's Secret.*  The secret of life is that there is no secret of life.

> —KURT M. PETERS, San Francisco, California

*Petty's Pronouncement on Personal Pacing.*  In order to finish first, you must first finish.

> —Race car driver RICHARD PETTY; from David Little

*Pierson's Law.*  If you're coasting, you're going downhill.

> —L. R. PIERSON, from "Rumsfeld's Rules," which appeared in the February 1977 *Washingtonian* magazine

*Pitt's Hypothesis.*  When things go wrong, there are always two faults, the second of which becomes apparent only after the first has been rectified.

> —UNKNOWN ORIGIN; from *Adhesives Age* magazine, March 1979

*Plato's Distinction.*  Man is a two-legged animal without feathers.

> —PLATO

*Pogo's Dictum.* A long run of good luck is a sure sign of bad luck.

>—POGO, a character from Walt Kelly's comic strip of the same
>name; from Michael L. Lazare, Armonk, New York

*Pompey's Law of Harassment.* If you are getting run out of town, get in front of the crowd and make it look like a parade.

>—SHERMAN LEE POMPEY, Florence, Oregon

*Popplewell's Law of Retirement.* Eat till you're sleepy. Sleep till you're hungry.

>—W. POPPLEWELL, Wills Point, Texas

*Povich's Rule on Dollars and Forgiveness.* Forgiveness is directly proportional to dollars—where there is big money there is big forgiveness.

>—Adapted from the *Washington Post*'s late sportswriter
>SHIRLEY POVICH quoting the "Fight Doctor" Ferdie Pacheco
>on July 3, 1997, referring to the second Tyson/Holyfield fight

*Powell's Law.* Never tell them what you won't do.

>—ADAM CLAYTON POWELL, cited by Julian Bond in a radio
>interview

*Prince Philip's Rule.* Never pass a bathroom.

>—THE DUKE OF EDINBURGH; from Robert J. T. Joy, M.D.,
>Bethesda, Maryland

*Priorities, Two Laws About.* (1) Nobody dies wishing they'd spent more time with their business. (2) Better to be a king for a night than a schmuck for a lifetime.

> —STEVE STINE, who heard the second from the character Rupert Pupkin (played by Robert De Niro) in the movie *King of Comedy*

*Probable Dispersal, Law of.* Whatever hits the fan will not be evenly distributed. (Sometimes called *The "How Come It All Landed on Me?" Law.*)

> —LOGICAL MACHINE CORP. AD, the *New Yorker*, 1976

*Proctor's Discovery.* Virtue is its own revenge.

> —MERT PROCTOR, in *Stars and Stripes*

*Professional's Law.* Doctors, dentists, and lawyers are only on time for appointments when you're not.

> —ROZANNE WEISSMAN, Washington, D.C.

*Pugsley's Revision.* Nobody's human.

> —M. E. PUGSLEY, Salt Lake City, Utah

*Quigley's Law.* Whoever has any authority over you, no matter how small, will attempt to use it.

—ANONYMOUS; received in an unmarked envelope

*Rabinowitz's Rule.* Let a smile be your umbrella, and you'll get a lot of rain in your face.

—GARY RABINOWITZ, a character in the TV show *Archie Bunker's Place;* from Tom Gill

*Rae's Dilemma.* When you move something to a better place for safekeeping, you can never remember the location of the better place.

—MRS. RAE P. JENSEN, San Francisco, California

*Ragucci's Truth of Love.* Love is exhausting.

—JOHN J. RAGUCCI, Everett, Massachusetts

*Rajneesh's Razor.* Experts consult; never wise men.

—SHREE RAJNEESH; from Shel Kagan

*Rapoport's Rule of the Roller-Skate Key.* Certain items which are crucial to a given activity will show up with uncommon regularity until the day when that activity is planned, at which point the item in question will disappear from the face of the earth.

　　—DAN RAPOPORT, Washington writer


*Ravage's Rule of Foot.* Excursions on foot will be approximately 58 percent uphill in both directions. This percentage will increase as the temperature rises.

　　—JOHN M. RAVAGE, Philadelphia, Pennsylvania


*Reach's Rule.* The secret of happiness is to let the other fellow do the worrying.

　　—A. J. REACH, of baseball and sporting goods fame, quoted in
　　the *Sporting News,* July 28, 1906


*Reynolds's Law.* It's just as easy to make a BIG mistake as a small one.

　　—JOAN A. REYNOLDS, Hyattsville, Maryland


*Rhy's Rule.* If it feels good, do it. If it doesn't feel good, do it anyway. It will feel good when it is over with.

　　—UNKNOWN ORIGIN; from James D. Haviland, Halifax, Nova
　　Scotia, who got it from a co-worker. He points out: "This one
　　. . . has gotten me through a number of unpleasant tasks,
　　including university."

*Rickover's Reminder.* At any moment during a twenty-four-hour day, only one-third of the people in the world are asleep. The other two-thirds are awake and creating problems.
> —ADM. HYMAN RICKOVER (1900–1986); from Jack Kime

*Rimmer's Law of Human Superiority.* The thing that sets us [human beings] apart from other animals is the fact that we do not clean our genitals with our own tongues.
> —From D. Reynolds, Golden Valley, Minnesota; quoting
> ARNOLD J. RIMMER, a character in the British comedy space-
> opera *Red Dwarf*

*Rives's Discovery.* Everything falls apart on the same day. (Rives calls this EFAOTS Day, and he pronounces it "E fouts.")
> —JOHN RIVES, Lafayette, Colorado

*Robertson's Law.* Everything happens at the same time with nothing in between.
> —UNKNOWN ORIGIN; from Paul Hebig, Chicago, who adds, "It
> usually refers to social engagements and business meetings."

*Roeper's Rules of the Universe.* A selection: (1) Gas station attendants are hired based on their lack of knowledge regarding directions. (2) All men look like geeks for seventy-two hours after a haircut. (3) You will not get the hiccups when you are alone. You will get the hiccups in the middle of your bar exam, or at a funeral, or on a first visit to your future in-laws' house. (4) If you think your pants have split, they have. (5) If you think your nylon has a run in it, it does. (6) The question you will be asked most often in your life is "Do you want fries with that?"

> —RICHARD ROEPER in the *Milwaukee Journal*, February 18, 1987; from Catherine Pfeifer

*Roger Jones's Laws of Life.* (1) Not everybody loves you. (2) Knowing that not everybody loves you means that you cannot please everybody.

> —ROGER B. JONES; from Neal Wilgus, Lubbock, Texas

*Rooke's Reminder.* Nothing is as simple as it seems.

> —WILLIAM ROOKE, Anaheim, California. The author uses this law when people call him to suggest a project that they insist is a "no-brainer."

*Rosenau's Law of Revolting Developments.* There will be at least one.

> —MILTON D. ROSENAU, JR., Santa Monica, California

*Rosoff's Rule of Thermodynamics.* A scalding hot cup of coffee will be too cool one instant after it has been adjudged to be at a drinkable temperature.

> —HENRY ROSOFF, APO, New York

***Rowe's Rule.*** The odds are six to five that the light at the end of the tunnel is a headlight of an oncoming express train.

—UNKNOWN ORIGIN

***Royal's Rule.*** Think lucky. If you fall in a pond, check your hip pockets for fish.

—University of Texas football coach DARRELL ROYAL

***Rubenstein's Rumination.*** If you're one in a million, there are 5,000 people like you.

—HAL RUBENSTEIN from *Nothing Goes With Nothing;* quoted by Michael Kesterton in his "Social Studies" column in the *Toronto Globe and Mail,* October 16, 1995

***Ruby's Remedy.*** The best bridge between despair and hope is a good night's sleep.

—HARRY RUBY, quoted in the *Reader's Digest,* July 1952

*Rudd's Universal Explanation.* Things like this happen.

 —UNKNOWN ORIGIN; from Ronald W. Tucker, Veracruz, Mexico

*Rudin's Law.* In a crisis that forces a choice to be made among alternative courses of action, most people will choose the worst one possible.

 —S. A. RUDIN of Atlanta, from a 1961 letter to the
  *New Republic*

*Ryan's Law.* Make three correct guesses consecutively and you will establish yourself as an expert.

 —UNKNOWN ORIGIN; from Robert Specht, Santa Monica,
  California

**Sacramento Manifesto.** When you're out to make your mark in the world, watch out for guys with erasers.

 —Spotted by TOM GILL on a T-shirt in the California capital

**Sailor's Dictum.** If you don't make waves, you're not under way.

 —LEONARD P. GOLLOBIN, Fairfax, Virginia

**Sam's Law.** Only fools can be certain; it takes wisdom to be confused.

 —SAM, a character in the TV show *Quincy*; from Steve Feinfrock

**Sanders's Law.** You never get walked on unless you throw yourself on the floor.

 —Chicago radio personality BETTY SANDERS

*Sandia Rules.* (1) I don't know what I want to hear until I hear what I don't want to hear. (2) The more important a thing is, the less time you are given to do it. (3) There are more ways to do something wrong than there are to do it right.

> —JAMES D. PLIMPTON, Albuquerque, New Mexico, who reports that they have been "floating around" Sandia National Labs for awhile

*Sattingler's Law.* It works better if you plug it in.

> —UNKNOWN ORIGIN; widely quoted

*Schroeder's Admonition.* Don't ask questions you don't want answers to.

> —CAPT. SCHROEDER, USCG; from W. R. Jurgens, Bowie, Maryland

*Seersucker Principle.* For every seer, there is a sucker.

> —From Steven Stine, who heard it in an old *Alfred Hitchcock Presents* rerun; a character played by Jack Klugman says it to a character played by E. G. Marshall.

*Seligson-Gerberg-Corman Rule of Sexual Sameness.* Having bad sex with someone you care about is the same as having bad sex with someone you don't care about.

> —MARCIA SELIGSON, MORT GERBERG, and AVERY CORMAN, from their *The Everything in the World That's the Same as Something Else Book*

*Sellen's Observation.* It doesn't take all kinds; we just have all kinds.

> —ROBERT W. SELLEN, Georgia State University, Atlanta, Georgia

*Sendak's Lament for the Rich.* There must be more to life than having everything.

> —MAURICE SENDAK

*Shadoon's Law.* If it's not one thing, it's ten.

> —DAN SHADOON, University of California, Davis; from Tom Gill

*Shoe-Shopper's Rule.* If it feels good, it's ugly. If it looks good, it hurts.

> —N. SALLY HASS, Sleepy Hollow, Illinois

*Sisley's Second Law.* We exist in a state of overcorrection.

*Sisley's Third Law.* Life is a soap opera, only a little slower.

*Sisley's Fourth Law.* The misdeeds of a member of any minority are attributed to all the persons in that minority, while the misdeeds of a member of the majority are attributed to that individual alone.

> —JOHN R. SISLEY, JR., Utica, New York, who notes, "Sisley has no first law. It is very much more impressive to begin with a second law."

*Slate's Law.* Growing old may be mandatory, but growing up is strictly optional.

> —CLAUDIA SLATE, Dallas, Texas

*Slevin's Rule.* The more a person is confused by what you say sincerely, the more likely they are to agree with you in principle.

> —MARTIN SLEVIN, Whitmore Park, Coventry, England

*Smith-Johannsen's Secret of Longevity.* Stay busy, get plenty of exercise, and don't drink too much. Then again, don't drink too little.

> —HERMAN "JACKRABBIT" SMITH-JOHANNSEN, 103-year-old Canadian cross-country skier, quoted in *Sports Illustrated,* August 21, 1978

***Smith's Rules.*** (1) You always pull the wrong shoelace first. (2) A Band-Aid string always pulls free before opening the wrapper. Once opened, the adhesive strips always stick together before the Band-Aid is applied.

> —DR. TERRY SMITH, Kirksville, Missouri, Northeast Missouri State University

***Smokler's Razor.*** The secret is not to learn something you don't want to practice.

> —MRS. SMOKLER, dairy-farm accountant who never learned how to milk a cow; quoted in the *Dallas Morning News,* August 16, 1998

***Sod's Law of Change.*** The more you want something to change, the more it stays the same. The more we want things to stay the same, the more they change.

> —JOHN EMSLEY in *New Scientist,* April 2, 1987

***Solberg's Saw.*** All progress isn't forward.

> —E. W. SOLBERG, Calimesa, California

***The Specialist's Law of Hole-Digging.*** It's a mighty sight better to have a little privy over a big hole than a big privy over a little hole.

> —CHARLES (CHIC) SALES in his best-selling book about outhouses, *The Specialist;* from Tom Gill, Lubbock, Texas

*Spring's Olfactory Axiom.* It doesn't smell until you step in it.

—BERNARD SPRING, D.D.S., Windsor, Ontario, Canada

*Stanton's Law of Minimum Requirements.* Bad breath is better than no breath at all.

—MARSHA STANTON, Dhahran, Saudi Arabia

*Stapley's Law for Young People.* Marry an ugly girl/boy; then in thirty years' time, you won't notice the difference as much.

—NIGEL STAPLEY, Dyfed, Wales

*Steckel's Rule to Success.* Good enough isn't good enough.

—PAUL W. STECKEL, Gainesville, Florida

*Steinert's Rule.* Whenever you need somebody, you can never find them, but when you don't need them you can't get rid of them.

—TERRELL W. STEINERT, San Francisco, California

*Stephens's Soliloquy.* Finality is death. Perfection is finality. Nothing is perfect. There are lumps in it.

—JAMES STEPHENS, quoted in *The Public Speaker's Treasure Chest*

*St. Murphy's Rule of Researching Religiously.* Read enough theological books and you will find someone who supports your beliefs. *Corollary.* Have enough Bible translations in your library and you will find one that agrees with what you think a particular passage says.

> —RON BIRK, San Marcos, Texas, from his longer list of
> St. Murphy's Commandments

*Stock's Observation.* You no sooner get your head above water than someone pulls your flippers off.

> —UNKNOWN ORIGIN; from Donald R. Woods

*Sutton's Laws.* (1) If at first you don't succeed, don't try again until you have successfully identified the bastards who are against you. (2) Extreme desirability never survives accrual.

> —FRANCIS W. A. SUTTON, St. Austell, Cornwall, U.K.

*Swartz's Maxim.* Live every day as if it were your last . . . and someday you'll be right.

> —UNKNOWN ORIGIN; radio call-in show

*Switzer's Embellishment.* You might remember that Mies van der Rohe said, "Less is more," which is true, more or less.

> —JOHN E. SWITZER, Bethesda, Maryland

*Sybert's Law.* Ignorance is blissful only to the intelligent.

—CHRISTOPHER SYBERT, Lutherville, Maryland

*Symons's Law of Flirting.* When a girl appears not to know you exist, it means she is definitely interested in you. Or that she is definitely uninterested in you. Or that she does not know you exist.

—DON SYMONS, Santa Barbara, California

*Szasz's Observation.* Why is it that when you are between seven and twelve, the children of your parents' friends are always of the opposite sex; but when you're between fifteen and twenty, they never are?

—FERENC M. SZASZ, Albuquerque, New Mexico

***Thanksgiving Thought from Ann Landers.*** Some of us should be thankful that we don't get what we deserve.

—ANN LANDERS, from her column of November 25, 1993

***Third Corollary.*** The difficulty of getting anything started increases exponentially with the number of people involved.

—JIM MACGREGOR; from Alan Otten

***Thoreau's Law.*** If you see a man approaching you with the obvious intent of doing you good, you should run for your life.

—Attributed to HENRY DAVID THOREAU (1817–1862) by
William H. Whyte, Jr., in *The Organization Man*

*Thorn's First Law of Return.* The closer the alumni live to the old hometown, the less likely they are to show up at the twentieth-anniversary reunion.

> —BILL THORN, quoted in Clarence Page's *Chicago Tribune* article on reunions, July 24, 1985

*Thurber's Amplification.* Love is blind, but desire just doesn't give a good goddamn.

> —JAMES THURBER, in his *Further Fables for Our Time*

*Tiedemann's Conclusion.* Procrastination is the root of all boredom.

> —JOANN TIEDEMANN, Tomahawk, Wisconsin

*Tillinger's Rule.* Moderation in all things, including moderation.

> —JUDY TILLINGER, New York City

*Tim's Admonition.* They can't chase you if you don't run.

> —PAT JETT, Hillsboro, Missouri, to her fourth-grade son, Tim, who was being chased at school by sixth graders

*Tom Jones's Law.* Friends may come and go, but enemies accumulate.

> —DR. THOMAS JONES, president of the University of South Carolina

*Tomlin's Request.* If love is the answer, could you rephrase the question?

—LILY TOMLIN, quoted in *Time,* March 28, 1977

*Townsend's Aphorisms.* (1) Anybody who can still do at sixty what he was doing at twenty wasn't doing much at twenty. (2) Marriage teaches you loyalty, forbearance, self-restraint, meekness, and a great many other things you wouldn't need if you had stayed single.

—JIMMY TOWNSEND, Georgia mountain philosopher, quoted in *Everything to Gain* by Jimmy and Rosalyn Carter

*Townsend's Law of Life.* Everybody wants to go to heaven, but nobody wants to die.

—O. J. BUD TOWNSEND, Canoga Park, California

*Tromberg's Truisms.* (1) The future isn't even here yet. (2) Aging simply means the present is shorter than the past and longer than the future.

—The late SHELLY TROMBERG, Washington, D.C.

*Truman's Triple Tenet.* Three things can ruin a man—money, power, and women. I never had any money. I never wanted power, and the only woman in my life is up at the house right now.

—HARRY S TRUMAN, quoted in *Scandals in the Highest Office,* by Hope Ridings Miller, 1973

*Truman's Truism.* When the "amens" get too loud in the back of the church, that's the time to go home and lock the smokehouse.

—HARRY S TRUMAN; forwarded by Nick Kass

*Truth-Seeker's Discovery.* (1) Time goes faster as we grow older because we need less time. (2) Time goes slower when we are young because we need more time (for things such as education, finding mate, learning job, and raising children).

—LINDA CEARBAUGH, Raleigh, North Carolina

*Tuppeny's Truism.* We are all in this alone.

—PEG TUPPENY, Chicago, Illinois

*The Turtle Principle.* If you go slow enough, long enough, you'll be in the lead again.

—WAYNE HOY, Rutgers University, Graduate School of Education; from Gerald Fava, Lake Hiawatha, New Jersey

*Udall's Observation on Discourse.* Everything that can be said about every subject has been said, just not everyone has said it.
—The late MORRIS K. UDALL

*Umbrella Law.* You will need three umbrellas: one to leave at the office, one to leave at home, and one to leave on the train.
—JAMES L. BLANKENSHIP, R. C. Auletta and Co., New York City

*Uncle Irving's Three Phases of Life.*
*First, youth.*
*Then middle age.*
*Then "Gee, you look wonderful."*
—Quoted by BOB LEVEY in the *Washington Post,*
September 3, 1979

*Unitas's Law.* If you hang around long enough, you'll end up somewhere.

 —Quarterback JOHNNY UNITAS, on being notified of his election
  to the Football Hall of Fame, January 29, 1979

*Unspeakable Law.* As soon as you mention something, if it's good, it goes away . . . if it's bad, it happens.

 —From ROBERT BLOCH's list in *The Book of Lists*

*Useful Refrain.* When you're down and out, lift up your voice and shout, "I'M DOWN AND OUT!"

 —UNKNOWN ORIGIN; sung to the compiler on a radio
  call-in show

***Van Roy's Laws.*** (1) Van Roy's Basic Law: Honesty is the best policy—there's less competition. (2) Rule of Empowerment at Work: Never agree with your boss until he says something. (3) Limitations Rule of Work Complexity: Anything that is simple to do is never easy to accomplish. (4) Self-Evident Marriage Motto: Marriage is like a bra—it's not really necessary but provides useful support. (5) Bruce's Wildest Dream Come True Law: I dreamed I invented sex and everyone had to pay me royalties. (6) Bruce's Sports Point: Rolling football gathers no score. (7) Bruce's Rule of Intelligent Manners: Never talk with your mouth full or your head empty. (8) Humanity's Self-Realization Rule from the Supreme Being: God gave us two ears and one mouth—maybe he was trying to tell us something. (9) Van Roy's Postulate: Love is like a pair of socks—you have to have two, and they gotta match.

—BRUCE W. VAN ROY, Vienna, Virginia

*Veeck's Law of Enforced Humility.*  When you've run as fast as you can up the highest mountain you can find, you will find something or somebody waiting at the top to deflate you.

—The late BILL VEECK in his 1962 book *Veeck—as in Wreck*

*Vernooy's Law of Psychopharmacology.*  The antidepressant medication that makes you feel like having sex again will cause anorgasmia (or impotence).

—DIANA VERNOOY, Teaneck, New Jersey

*The Viking Reminder.*  Always remember to pillage BEFORE you burn.

—UNKNOWN ORIGIN; from Bob Skole, Boston, Massachusetts, and Stockholm, Sweden

*Vito's Rule of Nonviolent Encounters.*  Never get in a battle of wits without ammunition.

—UNKNOWN ORIGIN; WRC radio

*Vogel's Nevers.*  Never attempt levity while filling out your insurance forms. Never think you can lose both gloves. Never get in a gunfight with seven men when you only have a six-shooter.

—W. J. VOGEL, Toppenish, Washington

*Volunteer's Law.*  If you dance with a grizzly bear, you had better let him lead.

  —From Stu Beck, Orleans, Massachusetts

*Vonnegut's Venting.*  Another flaw in the human character is that everybody wants to build and nobody wants to do maintenance.

  —KURT VONNEGUT in *Hocus Pocus;* from Neal Wilgus,
    Lubbock, Texas

*Walker's Law.* Associate with well-mannered persons and your manners will improve. Run with decent folk and your own decent instincts will be strengthened. Keep the company of bums and you will become a bum. Hang around with rich people and you will end by picking up the check and dying broke.

> —STANLEY WALKER, city editor of the *New York Herald-Tribune* during the 1930s

*Wall's Aphorism.* Survival is the ability to adapt to change.

> —GREGORY C. WALL, Carmel, Indiana

*The* Wall Street Journal *Rule.* In order to learn from mistakes, you have to first recognize you are making mistakes.

> —WALL STREET JOURNAL editorial, January 9, 1982

*Wareham's Rule.* Nobody says anything by accident.
> —JOHN WAREHAM in his 1980 book *Secrets of a Corporate Headhunter*

*Warren's Dilemma.* Life ain't worth living, but what else can you do with it?
> —GRACE A. WARREN, Sacramento, California

*Warren's Words of Wisdom.* There's a lot to be said for brevity.
> —RUSSELL WARREN; from Terry B. Smith, Kirksville, Missouri

*Wearing Hats, Law of.* Never wear a hat that has more character than you do.
> —Hatmaker MICHAEL HARRIS; from Bill Spivey, San Francisco, California

*Weiner's Wisdom.* Indecision is the key to flexibility.
> —LT. T. F. WEINER, USN; from R. J. Montore, Henderson, Kentucky

*Weissman's Discovery.* When a man says he is "separated," it means he hasn't seen his wife since breakfast.
> —ROZANNE WEISSMAN, Washington, D.C.

*Wells's Law.* When in doubt, use clout.
> —STEPHEN B. WELLS, New Canaan, Connecticut

*West's Latest Discoveries.* Social sobriquet: The cream rises to the top; unfortunately, so does the scum.

—ROY W. WEST, Philadelphia, Pennsylvania

*West's Time Constant.* A split second is the time that elapses between the moment you step into a perfectly adjusted shower and someone turns on the washing machine and the dishwasher and flushes every toilet in the house.

—The late ROBERT TREE WEST, Minneapolis, Minnesota

*Whispered Rule.* People will believe anything if you whisper it.

—FARMERS' ALMANAC, 1978 edition

*White's Certainties.* (1) Anybody who tells you he is shy isn't. (2) People who use your first name in every other sentence cannot be trusted. (3) Anybody who refers to himself in the third person is over-paid. (4) When somebody says "ironically" she means "coincidentally." (5) Despite advertising claims, there is no such thing as an odor-free litter box. (6) *Star Search* will never find a star.

—DIANE WHITE, the *Boston Globe*

*Whitney's Second Law of the Democratic Process.* In a democracy, having been born, death ensues. Everything else is negotiable.

—PETER WHITNEY, Tucson, Arizona

*Wilcox's Law.*  A pat on the back is only a few centimeters from a kick in the pants.

——UNKNOWN ORIGIN; from Robert Specht

*Wilgus's Warning.*  Always slow down for Dead Man's Curve.

——NEAL WILGUS, Lubbock, Texas

*Willets on Aging.*  There is an engaging legend abroad in the land that advancing years mellow one and somehow bring out the kindliest impulses of one's nature, that the countryside swarms with repentant Scrooges. My own observation has been that when a bastard grows old, he simply becomes an old bastard.

——ISABEL M. WILLETS, LeClaire, Iowa

*Wilson's First Three Life Lessons.*  (1) Liquid shoe polish doesn't work. (2) A man who wants time to read and write must let the grass grow long. (3) Beware of people who are always well dressed.

——SLOAN WILSON, in *What Shall We Wear to the Party? The Man in the Gray Flannel Suit Twenty Years Before and After;* from Daniel Humphreys, Cincinnati

*Wing-Walking, First Law of.*  Never leave hold of what you've got until you've got hold of something else.

——DONALD HERZBERG, dean of Georgetown University's graduate school. It came from the days of the barnstorming pilots and is now applied in situations such as when one quits a job before having another lined up.

*Winkler's Rule.* Assumptions are the termites of relationships.
  —Actor HENRY WINKLER in his Emerson College graduation speech, June 1995

*Winner's Law.* It isn't whether you win or lose, but how much you win by.
  —PAUL J. SPREITZER, age fifteen, Chicago, Illinois

*Winters's Rule.* In a crowded place, the person directly behind you always has the loudest voice. *Corollary.* People with loud voices never have anything interesting to say.
  —CHRISTINE WINTERS, the *Chicago Tribune*

*Wolfe's Rule.* There is nothing that can make one look younger than being younger.
  —DORIS WOLFE, Springfield, Missouri

*Wolf's Law.* You never get a second chance to make a first impression.
  —UNKNOWN ORIGIN; from N. D. Butler

*Wolpe's Law of Mortality.* If you live long enough, something will kill you.

— BRUCE C. WOLPE, North Sydney, Australia

*Woman's Equation.* Whatever women do, they must do twice as well as men to be thought half as good. Luckily, this is not difficult.

— UNKNOWN ORIGIN; from Robert Specht

*Wright's Perspective.* Give me the luxuries of life and I will willingly do without the necessities.

— FRANK LLOYD WRIGHT; from Bernard L. Albert

*Yauger's Law of Backstabbing.* When you talk about someone behind their back, their back will be right behind you.

—DAVID YAUGER, Leesburg, Virginia

*Yearwood's Admonition.* To err is human, but do not use up the eraser before the pencil.

—R. L. YEARWOOD, Hereford, Texas

*Yoakum's Rule.* Don't put off until tomorrow what you can get done sometime next week.

—ROBERT YOAKUM, *Yoakum Features,* Lakeville, Connecticut

*Yolen's Law of Self-Praise.* Proclaim yourself "World Champ" of something—tiddlywinks, rope-jumping, whatever—send this notice to newspapers, radio, TV, and wait for challengers to confront you. Avoid challenges as long as possible, but continue to send news of your achievements to all media. Also, develop a newsletter and letterhead for communications.

> —WILL YOLEN, former PR man and kite VIP, who by now probably owns a suitcase filled with clippings of articles that talk about him and his World Championship.

**Zais's First Postulate.** As long as you retain the capacity to blush, your immortal soul is in no particular danger.

> —ELLIOT ZAIS, Corvallis, Oregon

**Zimmerman's Corollary.** Looking competent is just as effective as being competent.

> —JOHN A. MATTSEN

**Zisla's Law.** If you're asked to join a parade, don't march behind the elephants.

> —HAROLD ZISLA, South Bend, Indiana

# AFTERWORDS

This is the eighth work in a series of books that will help describe elements of the real world through laws, rules, principles, and maxims. More are planned.

Needless to say, the Director is ever eager to collect new laws and hear from readers in care of:

Box 80

Garrett Park, MD 20896-0080

e-mail: newdefiner@aol.com

Shortly after the first *Official Rules* was published in 1978, the Director got a letter from a good woman from Pagosa Springs, Colorado, who said: "Once discovered, *The Official Rules* is like sex, indispensable."

Ever since then the Director has relished the task of going to the mailbox for the Center's mail.

One of the benefits that accrue to those who help the Murphy Center with its research is their appointment as a fellow of the Murphy Center. The value of such a title should be reckoned by the fact that it can be given only by the Director and cannot be bought (at least not cheaply) and cannot be taken away by anyone but the Director (who has yet to decommission a Fellow). There are now so many Fellows that it would be impossible to list all of them at the end of the book—as was the practice in earlier Center publications.

In addition, there is a select group of people who have contributed so much to the work of the Center over the last twenty years that they have achieved the rank of Senior Fellow. They cannot be thanked enough; but I will do it one more time: the late Theodore C. Achilles, Joseph E. Badger, Charles Boyle, Nancy Dickson, the late Russell Dunn, Sr., Fred Dyer, M. Mack Earle, John Ehrman, Tom Gill, Joseph C. Goulden, John Hagemann, Shel Kagan, Edward Logg, Martin Kottmeyer, Herbert H. Paper, the late Charles D. Poe, Frank S. Preston, Conrad Schneiker, Bob and Monika Skole, Marshall L. Smith, Robert D. Specht, Steve Stine, Gregg Townsend, the late Robert T. West, Neal Wilgus, Bennett Willis, Jr., Jack Womeldorf, Steve Woodbury, and Donald R. Woods.

# INDEX

**Greed & Excess.** Baber's Rule, Brauer's Warning, Dato's Law, Great American Axiom, Midas's Law, Sendak's Lament for the Rich

**Happiness.** Lin's Maxim, Reach's Rule

**Honesty.** Parsons's Honesty Rule, Van Roy's Laws

**Human Nature.** Albert's Law of the Sea, Allen's Lament, Boucher's Observations, Dale's Dictum, David's Law of Habits, Dunlop's Determination, Ertz's Observation on Immortality, Gage's Rule, Hartig's "How Is Good Old Bill?" "We're Divorced" Law, Hartig's "Sleeve in the Cup, Thumb in the Butter" Law, Lowell's Constant, Meier's Law, Mencken's Meta-law, Nestor's Law, Newman's Law, Quigley's Law, Reynolds's Law, Rimmer's Law of Human Superiority, Seersucker Principle, Sellen's Observation, Sisley's Fourth Law, Stock's Observation, Third Corollary, Townsend's Law of Life, Vonnegut's Venting, Winters's Rule, Yearwood's Admonition

**Humility.** Glasow's Law, Veeck's Law of Enforced Humility

**Humor.** Amis's Reminder, Black's Discovery, Elsner's Observations, The Murphy Validity Proof

**Ignorance.** Bentov's Law, Moos's Law, Sybert's Law

**Incompetence.** Akre's Axiom, Akre's Corollary, Fuchs's Fact

**Intelligence.** Alex's Iron Axiom, Fraraccio's Law, James's Distinction, Kiesel's Railroading Analogy, Sybert's Law

**Irony.** Ann's Law of Inevitability, Armstrong's Collection Law, Ash's Axiom, Berla's Version, Daniel's Delight, Dr. Hayes's Hint, Elsner's Observation, Gamson's Geriatric Corollary to Newton's Laws of Gravity, Gwinns Theory of Necessity, Herblock's Law, Igbara's Equation, Neuhaus's Rule, Petersen's Postulate, Steinert's Rule, Thorn's First Law of Return, White's Certainties

**Knowledge & Wisdom.** Bishop's Theorem, Boatman's Law,

Landers's Revision, Rajneesh's Razor, Ryan's Law, Sam's Law

**Lament.** Cohen's Law, Eliot's Observation, Kidd's Enlightenment, Mame's Lament

**Life.** Addis's Elaboration of Forrest Gump's Simile, Adler's Explanation, Agnes Allen's Law, Alex's Iron Axiom, Balzer's Law, Billings's Realization, Borstelmann's Rule, Boyle's Laws, Cooper's Discovery, Coper's Complaint, Gandhi's Observation, Greene's Law, Hovancik's "Wait till Tomorrow" Principle, Hungarian Proverb, Jump's Discovery, Lamb's Law, Lowell's Law of Life, Mame's Lament, McCarthy's Realization, Mintz's Law, Miz Beaver's Summation of Walt Kelly's Philosophy, Peters's Secret, Rives's Discovery, Rosenau's Law of Revolting Developments, Sisley's Third Law, Tuppeny's Truism, Warren's Dilemma

**Love.** Brown's Revision, Daugherty's List of Things a Person Should Never Say, Frankenfeld's Revised Proverbs, Fraser's Additions, Miller's Principle, Ragucci's Truth of Love, Thurber's Amplification, Tomlin's Request

**Luck.** Dorothea's Comforting Thought for the Day, McDougal's Law, Pogo's Dictum

**Marriage.** Alexander's Rules, Carvlin's Commentary, Igbara's Equation, Mary's Rule, Neudal's Law, Townsend's Aphorisms, Van Roy's Laws, Weissman's Discovery

**Memory.** Hasselbring's Law, Rae's Dilemma

**Men.** Adams's Law, Beifield's Principle, Broome's Discovery, Carol's Rule, Gooden's Rule, Jennifer's Law, Mary's Rule, Mother Sigafoo's Observation, Payne's Observation

**Money & Wealth.** Armstrong's Collection Law, Baird's Law, Boyle's Laws, Budri's Generalizations, DeCaprio's Rule, Gold's Law, Issawi on Sex and Money, Pardo's Postulates, Povich's Rule on Dollars and Forgiveness, Sendak's Lament for the Rich, Truman's Triple